FORENSICS

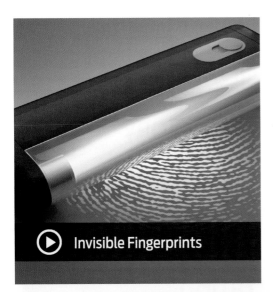

Invisible Fingerprints

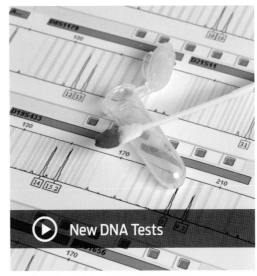

New DNA Tests

The Science of Broken Glass Solves Crimes

STEM IN CURRENT EVENTS

FORENSICS

By John Perritano

MASON CREST

Mason Crest
450 Parkway Drive, Suite D
Broomall, PA 19008
www.masoncrest.com

© 2017 by Mason Crest, an imprint of National Highlights, Inc.

Printed and bound in the United States of America.

First printing
9 8 7 6 5 4 3 2 1

Series ISBN: 978-1-4222-3587-4
ISBN: 978-1-4222-3592-8
ebook: 978-1-4222-8293-9

Produced by Shoreline Publishing Group
Designer: Tom Carling, Carling Design Inc.
Production: Sandy Gordon
www.shorelinepublishing.com

Front cover: Dreamstime: Bizpix tl; Tossi66 tr. Shutterstock/Payless images b.

Library of Congress Cataloging-in-Publication Data

Names: Perritano, John, author.
Title: Forensics / by John Perritano.
Description: Broomall, PA : Mason Crest, [2017] | Series: STEM in current   events | Includes index.
Identifiers: LCCN 2016004800| ISBN 9781422235928 (hardback) | ISBN 9781422235874 (series) | ISBN
    9781422282939 (ebook)
Subjects: LCSH: Forensic sciences--Juvenile literature.
Classification: LCC HV8073.8 .P468 2017 | DDC 363.25--dc23
LC record available at http://lccn.loc.gov/2016004800

Contents

Key Icons to Look For

Words to Understand: These words with their easy-to-understand definitions will increase the reader's understanding of the text, while building vocabulary skills.

Sidebars: This boxed material within the main text allows readers to build knowledge, gain insights, explore possibilities, and broaden their perspectives by weaving together additional information to provide realistic and holistic perspectives.

Educational Videos: Readers can view videos by scanning our QR codes, providing them with additional educational content to supplement the text. Examples include news coverage, moments in history, speeches, iconic sports moments, and much more!

Text-Dependent Questions: These questions send the reader back to the text for more careful attention to the evidence presented here.

Research Projects: Readers are pointed toward areas of further inquiry connected to each chapter. Suggestions are provided for projects that encourage deeper research and analysis.

Series Glossary of Key Terms: This back-of-the-book glossary contains terminology used throughout this series. Words found here increase the reader's ability to read and comprehend higher-level books and articles in this field.

Into the destruction and the mess of a crime scene steps a team of experts in forensic science. They'll use the latest technology and gear to sift through the evidence and point detectives toward the criminals.

INTRODUCTION
Crime Stoppers

Words to Understand

ballistics   the study of firearms and projectiles, including bullets

genetic   relating to a person's heredity

high-resolution   providing detailed images that have a high number of pixels per inch

toxicology   scientific study of poisons

A December morning started out hot and hazy in Sydney, Australia. With 10 days until Christmas, many people were in a manic frame of mind. They scurried across the city buying Christmas presents, planning parties, and decorating for the holidays.

As dawn turned into late morning, a few people decided to begin their day quietly before setting about their daily grind. John O'Brien, 83, visited the Lindt Café in the middle of the city's business district after his annual eye doctor's appointment. Louisa Hope, 50, and her mother, Robyn, 70, had stayed overnight in Sydney and went to the café as a side trip. Workers behind the café's counter busily filled orders.

At about 9:44 A.M., a man who had been sitting at a table pulled out a gun and held it to the head of the cafe's manager. The man, Haron Monis, then yelled for everyone to stand with their hands in the air. This was a terrorist attack, he yelled. He claimed to be a member of the Islamic State, also known as ISIS, a terrorist organization in the Middle East. Monis, wearing camouflage pants and a baseball cap, said he had placed bombs in the restaurant. Everyone, he shouted, should do as he said. It was the beginning of a 16-hour siege with the police.

The next morning, at around two o'clock, police stormed the café using flash grenades. The grenades exploded with an ear-splitting bang, sending a bright flash of light into the café, stunning everyone inside. The police found Monis and shot him dead. The carnage was over in about 30 seconds. Two others in the café also died.

Scanning the Scene

The restaurant was now a crime scene. A forensics investigation, run by the New South Wales Coroner's office, began. As part of their investigation, officials decided to use a new, highly sophisticated tool to reconstruct the crime. Known as High Definition Surveying, or HDS, investigators examined the café using computerized 3D scanners that broke the crime scene down into reams of digital information.

Laser scanners swept over the inside of the café mapping and measuring nearly every square inch. Crime scene investigators used handheld scanners to capture **high-resolution** images

01

Among the newest devices being used by forensic teams is a 360-degree scanner like this one that creates a complete view of a crime scene for later analysis.

of blood splatters. They then put photographs over the scans, rendering a virtual, yet realistic, view of the crime scene.

The scans allowed experts to see where each person was located during the shootout, including police. Investigators also followed the 3D evidence to see where each shot was fired and where the victims fell. Police planned to take all that information and plug it into a 3D printer, allowing them to re-create evidence that they could then pick up and examine.

HDS gave forensic investigators the ability to see what exactly occurred during the shootout. "All of a sudden we're back at the crime scene, where people were, where the projectiles were, looking at the explosions, looking at **ballistics**," said police officer Scott Weber.

Father of Forensic Science

Long before TV shows *CSI* and *Bones*, the fictional detective Sherlock Holmes was the first to make forensics popular. *The Adventures of Sherlock Holmes*, written by Arthur Conan Doyle, so inspired French criminologist Edmond Locard that he decided to build a crime lab in Paris to study crime scene evidence. Locard, known as the Father of Forensic Science, said criminals always leave bits of clues at a crime scene.

Solving the Crime

High Definition Surveying is just one of the latest tools used by forensic scientists to take the guesswork out of criminal cases. Although forensic science has been around in one form or another for hundreds of years, we live today in a golden age of forensics, dominated by new science and mind-boggling technology.

At its core, forensics is the scientific method of gathering and examining evidence that prosecutors can then use in a court of law. It encompasses such disciplines as **toxicology**, ballistics, and fingerprints. It also includes DNA profiling, which uses variations in a person's **genetic** code not only to identify individuals and put them behind bars, but also to clear those wrongly convicted of a crime.

Much More

Not only is forensics used to enforce the law, but scientists also use it to protect public health and to tell who is right and wrong in civil disputes. Some scientists use forensics to piece together the past when they discover age-old bones and artifacts. Other scientists study how and why buildings, bridges, and other structures collapse into heaps of dust, brick, and steel.

Still, it is in the world of crime where forensics has captured the public's imagination. A drop of blood, a bit of skin, or a carpet fiber that shouldn't be where it is, can send a person to jail—or to the death chamber.

 Text-Dependent Questions

1. What is high-definition surveying, and how is it used?

2. Who is considered the Father of Forensic Science?

3. Name three ways forensic science is used today.

 Research Project

Rent, download, or just watch any movie or TV show related to crime scene investigations, including movies such as *The Bone Collector* or *Murder by Numbers*. You can also read a detective novel. As you watch and read, answer these questions on a separate sheet of paper:

1. How was the crime scene protected?

2. What type of forensic evidence did investigators collect?

3. What methods did investigators use to tie the evidence to the crime scene?

Chemistry is just one of the many scientific disciplines called on in the world of forensics. Here, an analyst tests a sample from a crime scene to find out if it's blood . . . or not.

SCIENCE AND
Forensics

Words to Understand

anthropology   study of humans in all aspects, including development, sociology, and culture

electrons   negatively charged atomic particles

entomology   study of insects

enzymes   chemicals produced by living cells that control various chemical reactions

ionizing   process by which an atom loses or gains electrons and acquires an electrical charge

Forensic science is much more than DNA, fingerprints, blood, and ballistics. It includes many scientific disciplines, such as psychology, **anthropology**, criminalistics, dentistry, and **entomology**, among others.

Forensic psychology is one of the most well known of all the forensic sciences, the place where mind meets criminal. Forensic psychologists, sometimes known as "profilers," delve into the psyches of criminals, trying to figure out their identity or to anticipate their next move.

What is a Forensic Psychologist?

Popular movies and TV shows such as *Silence of the Lambs* and *Profiler* have highlighted the work of forensic psychologists. These experts are often asked to determine the mental health of an accused criminal before that person stands trial.

While the forensic psychologist deals chiefly with the living, it is the job of the forensic pathologist to study the dead and determine how they succumbed. A person can die suddenly, unexpectedly, violently, or suspiciously. The pathologist must pinpoint how, when, and where a person died. Most pathologists work as public officials, for governments, states, counties, towns, and cities. They are coroners or medical examiners. Others work privately and are paid a fee to investigate a death.

Forensic anthropologists study decomposed human remains hoping to find clues relating to a person's identity and death. Police also call upon the forensic anthropologist to determine whether a crime has occurred. A forensic dentist studies teeth as a means of identification.

Criminalists are the men and women working in the laboratory comparing, identifying, and interpreting physical evidence taken from the crime scene. A forensic entomologist is perhaps the creepiest forensic job. He or she looks for clues by studying insects on, near, or inside, a corpse.

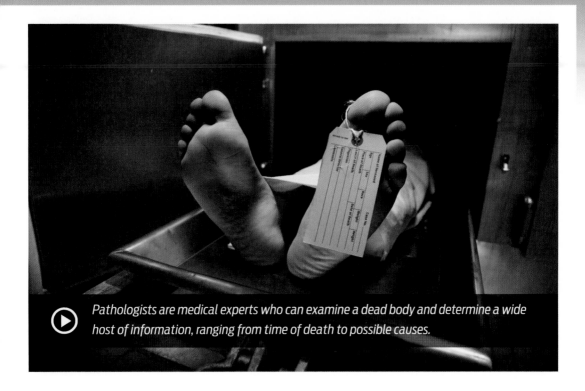

Pathologists are medical experts who can examine a dead body and determine a wide host of information, ranging from time of death to possible causes.

Talking to the Dead

Trying to understand what a corpse has to say is at the center of most forensic work. Dead men and women do tell tales. All a forensic scientist has to do is listen. Listening, however, can be difficult, especially if scientists cannot find a victim. That's where cutting-edge science can help.

Criminals often bury their victims, creating a formidable hurdle for law enforcement. Criminals have buried the dead in a variety of places, including in swamps, under garages, inside bridge pilings, and alongside houses.

The longer a corpse is buried, the harder it becomes to find. In fact, the Federal Bureau of Investigation (FBI) says most of these gruesome graveyards tend to be four to six years old by the time police locate them. A body buried for so long yields few clues. Animals destroy evidence, or rain and snow wash it away.

Most of those buried are hidden at an average depth of 1.5 to 2.5 feet (45 to 76 cm). The corpses are usually face down and wrapped in cloth or in plastic. All of this makes finding a buried corpse difficult. Yet, there are several ways that forensic scientists can pinpoint the location of a grave.

As a body decomposes, it releases gases. In most cases, law enforcement agencies use trained dogs to sniff out the dead. The dogs have an uncanny ability to detect the scents created by a decomposing corpse. In other cases, forensic scientists call on botanists (scientists who study plants), entomologists, and even geologists to assist.

Forensic scientists can now use a new tool, a hand-held odor-sniffing device called LABRADOR, which is short for Lightweight Analyzer for Buried Remains and Decomposition Odor Recognition.

Two Paths to Decay

As soon as a person dies, the body begins to decay, a process called decomposition. The rate of decay follows two different paths. The first is *autolysis*, in which the **enzymes** in the body's cells begin to meltdown. The hotter it gets, the faster the body decomposes.

The second path is *putrefaction*. This is the process by which bacteria escape from inside the body's intestinal tract. Following a rigid timetable, the escaping bacteria give the corpse's neck, abdomen, shoulders, and head a greenish look. The body then fills up with gas as bacteria feast on fetid flesh and tissue. Eventually skin will blister, hair will fall out and fingernails will sink back into the fingers.

Sniffing Out a Crime

Developed by scientists at the Oak Ridge National Laboratory in Tennessee, LABRADOR can sniff for 30 classes of chemicals given off by a rotting corpse. The device is so sensitive that it can outsmell a cadaver dog. It can even alert investigators to the type and amount of odor present.

"In other words, it can map the odor plume coming from the ground where the body is buried, which can be a key factor in pinpointing the location of the grave or looking for victims in natural disasters," said Oak Ridge forensic expert Arpad A. Vass, who helped build LABRADOR.

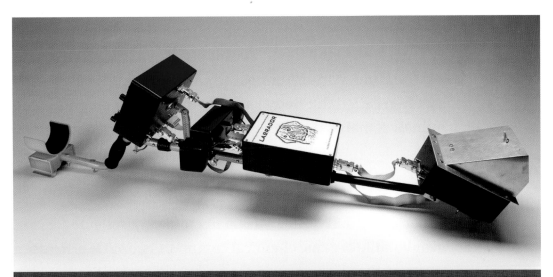

This LABRADOR device uses chemical analysis of the molecules that create odor or smell to help discover the location of dead bodies.

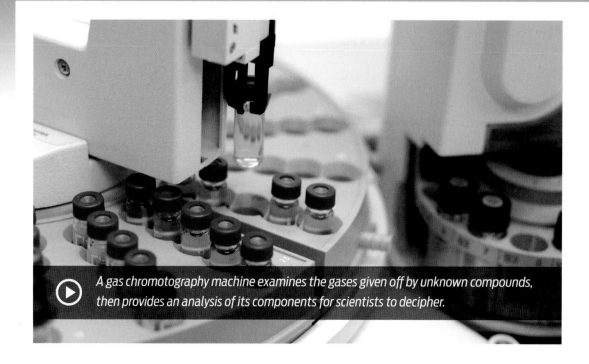

A gas chromotography machine examines the gases given off by unknown compounds, then provides an analysis of its components for scientists to decipher.

Before Vass and his colleagues could engineer LABRADOR, they had to figure out just what chemicals, and in what percentages, a human body emits as it decomposes. Vass was lucky. He works at the University of Tennessee's Anthropological Research Facility, often called the Body Farm. At the farm, scientists study how human remains decompose over time.

Volatile Compounds

Over a period of four years, Vass painstakingly collected gases, known as volatile organic chemical compounds, or VOCs. He used special traps that he put over the graves of four decomposing bodies buried 18 inches (45 cm) deep. It took about 17 days for VOCs to penetrate the surface of the ground, allowing the traps to collect the gases.

Vass then put each sample through a gas chromatography mass spectrometry (GC/MS) machine. The GC/MS bombarded the gas samples with a beam of **electrons**, **ionizing** the atoms. The ions were then blasted out of a vacuum chamber, striking a magnetic field. As a result, the ions fanned out in a spectrum, separating the gases into specific layers like light through a glass prism.

A computer then analyzed which atoms were in the gases. Vass concluded that a decomposing body produces eight major classes of chemicals containing 478 specific volatile compounds. Of that amount, he identified 30 compounds specifically associated with human decomposition.

Although cadaver dogs do a great job finding the dead (they can even find human remains hundreds of years old), they cannot tell the concentration of gas coming from a burial site. LABRADOR can. Moreover, by analyzing the results obtained by the device, pathologists can figure out how long a person has been dead.

Success!

The device was used successfully in 2010 to find the body of Lynsie Ekelund, a student at Fullerton College in California. Ekelund had been missing for nine years. Detectives knew she was buried somewhere on a 40-acre (16 ha) ranch, but her location proved elusive. They then brought in LABRADOR to pinpoint the exact location. The machine told them where to look. Crime scene investigators started digging 50 feet (15.2 m) from where they ultimately found the girl's body.

Notable Achievements in Forensic Science

1807

The University of Edinburgh in Scotland forms one of the first schools for the study of forensics.

1880

Scottish physician Henry Faulds first suggests that police can use fingerprints to identify criminals.

1927

Dr. Calvin Goddard and his partner, Philip Gravelle, invent the comparison microscope, allowing police to compare the markings on bullets side-by-side.

1932

The Federal Bureau of Investigation (FBI) opens its crime laboratory.

1986

Prosecutors in Great Britain use DNA evidence for the first time to identify a suspect, Colin Pitchfork, as the murderer of two young girls.

1987

Prosecutors, using DNA evidence for the first time in the United States, win a conviction against Tommy Lee Andrews for assaulting several people in Orlando, Florida.

Hair-Raising Science

In the fall of 2000, two hunters walking along the south shore of the Great Salt Lake in Utah made a grisly discovery. They found a shallow grave 30 yards (27.4 m) or so from Interstate 80. Inside the grave was a bag. Inside the bag was a white sock, a T-shirt, a human skull, 12 bones, and several strands of hair. There was no wallet or purse. No driver's license. No identification of any kind.

The body was badly decomposed. Dental records, often used to identify victims, proved useless. Time ticked slowly away. A cold case grew more frigid by the day. For years, investigators called the woman "Saltair Sally" because of where her remains were discovered.

Then in 2007, the state medical examiner decided to give the investigation another look. He gave a sample of the hair found in the bag to scientists at a Salt Lake City-based company called IsoForensics.

The company's scientists took the blonde hair and put it through a brand new

Whose hair is it? Under the microscope, hair strands provide forensic scientists with a wealth of data, even including what the former hair owner might have eaten.

technique, isotopic hair analysis, developed by researchers at the University of Utah. Isotopes are versions of the same element but with different numbers of neutrons (atomic particles with no electrical charge). The more neutrons an isotope has, the heavier it is. In other words, it has a heavier atomic mass than the element would normally have.

Everything is composed of isotopes, even hair, which has carbon, nitrogen, and sulfur isotopes. The isotopes find their way there by the food we eat and the water we drink.

Scientists focused their attention on the levels of hydrogen and oxygen isotopes in the woman's hair. These isotopes are found in water and vary from place to place. Isotopes found in hair can tell police where someone might have drunk water and lived, weeks or even years before his or her death.

The analysis proved eye opening. Scientists said two years prior to her death, the woman was constantly moving. She was in a region much like Salt Lake City. She then moved west, and then northwest. She did this several times before her death.

Police took this information and did some old-fashioned gum-shoe work. They found a missing person's report for a woman identified as Nikole Bakoles. On a hunch, forensic scientists

In a large model, DNA strands look like this, but at the microscopic level, they build our bodies into what we are. Forensic scientists use DNA to identify specific humans.

also took a sample of the woman's DNA and compared it to her mother's DNA. It was a match. "Saltair Sally" now had a name, a face, and a family.

Niki, as her parents called her, indeed moved as scientists said she did. She traveled from Salt Lake City to Seattle, Washington. Niki and her family eventually fell out of touch, and she was last seen living in a hotel near Salt Lake City with her boyfriend in March 2000. The missing person's report was filed three years later.

Despite identifying the remains, police did not make an arrest in the case. Still, Niki's family was able to bury her remains and find some closure. "For the last twelve years, every day I've been worried about her: 'Is she safe? Does she have a place to stay? Is she eating properly? Is someone abusing her?'" Nancie Bakoles, Niki's mother told a local TV station. "That's the good part, putting that to rest."

Smile! You're on DNA Camera

During the mid-1980s, a revolution occurred in forensic science when researchers found a way to use genes to solve crimes and identify people. They called it DNA profiling. DNA is short for deoxyribonucleic acid, a spiral-shaped molecule of chemicals containing a person's genes, the material that determines in-herited characteristics such as eye and hair color. DNA is found in the body's cells.

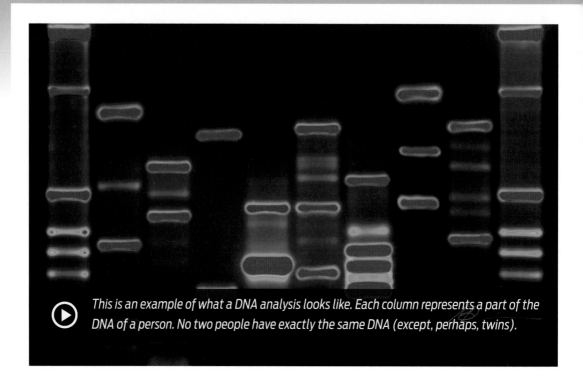

This is an example of what a DNA analysis looks like. Each column represents a part of the DNA of a person. No two people have exactly the same DNA (except, perhaps, twins).

While most of the information contained in DNA is the same in every person, certain parts of DNA are unique to each individual. Scientists are able to remove those parts of the DNA from sweat, blood, saliva, and hair left at a crime scene.

Now scientists have taken DNA profiling to a new level, putting a face to the molecule with a process called DNA phenotyping. It allows scientists to create a three-dimensional image of a person's face—a genetic mug shot. Inside a person's DNA is a file cabinet stuffed with the genetic information that determines a person's physical characteristics. This file cabinet (a "DNA blueprint") is locked away in every cell of the body. Researchers can use the genetic markers found in a drop of blood or a bit of saliva to open up that cabinet. The information is then plugged into a computer with special software. Within minutes, the software rapidly draws connections between the genetic information and points on a face. It then sketches out an image of what that person might look like.

 Text-Dependent Questions

1. Explain the process of putrefaction.

2. What are volatile organic compounds?

3. What year did U.S. prosecutors win their first criminal case using DNA evidence?

 Research Project

Break off into groups of three or four. Collect three types of hair: dog, cat, and human. Next, tape a sample of each hair to a microscope slide. Place each slide under a microscope. (You can find one in your school's science lab.) Create a chart that compares each sample. Write down the source of the hair, its color, and whether each is straight or curly. What does the medulla (inner layer of the hair shaft) and the cuticle (the outer part of the hair shaft) look like? Discuss your findings.

 Step one: Seal it off. Making sure that a crime scene is not "contaminated" by the presence of people outside of the investigation is a vital first step in forensics.

TECHNOLOGY AND
Forensics

Words to Understand

density   a measure of a quantity of mass

epilepsy   a medical disorder of the brain that involves episodes of irregular electrical discharges

manslaughter   the spontaneous and unlawful killing of one person by another

vaporizes   turns to gas

The killing of 10-year-old Damilola Taylor in 2000 shocked Great Britain. His family had just moved to London from Nigeria seeking a better life. Damilola's parents also hoped the move would help their son get treatment for a severe case of **epilepsy**.

One fall day, Damilola was leaving the library on his way home. As he walked, a gang of youths attacked him, stabbing the boy in the leg with a broken beer bottle. Damilola bled to death.

Police arrested several suspects, but prosecutors were unable to win convictions. Part of the problem was that police had missed a bloodstain on a sneaker belonging to one of the accused. The case took a circuitous route through the courts. It wasn't until 2006 that two brothers were convicted of **manslaughter**. Had the blood evidence been found earlier, experts say, perhaps Damilola's killers would have faced justice sooner.

If the crime occurred today, scientists could use a new technology, hyperspectral imaging, which can detect hard-to-see splatters of blood. The process has the ability to revolutionize crime scene investigations.

Trail of Blood

In the world of forensics, blood has been, and continues to be, the most important type of physical evidence. The existence of blood where it shouldn't be usually means something bad, or out of the ordinary, has happened. Blood's presence links suspects with victims and can be more incriminating than an eyewitness account. A bloodstain or a blood splatter can tell police volumes, such as where people were standing during a crime, and who did the actual killing. Blood never lies.

Still, finding traces of blood can be difficult. Searching is tedious and time consuming. Sometimes, blood evidence is not easy to locate. Stains might not be readily visible.

Scientists at Teesside University in Great Britain found a way to detect tiny blood stains that could not be seen with existing technology. They can also date months-old blood to within one day, helping investigators determine when a person might have died or, at least, when that person might have been injured.

Here's how hyperspectral imaging technology works. Humans can see only three bands of visible light: red, green, and blue. However, light is made up of many more colors. Spectral imaging divides these colors into a spectrum that covers a wide range of wavelengths that humans cannot see.

Scientists, led by Dr. Meeze Islam, a physical chemist, developed a device with a liquid-crystal filter. The device scans an area like a camera does. The filter acts like a prism, isolating different

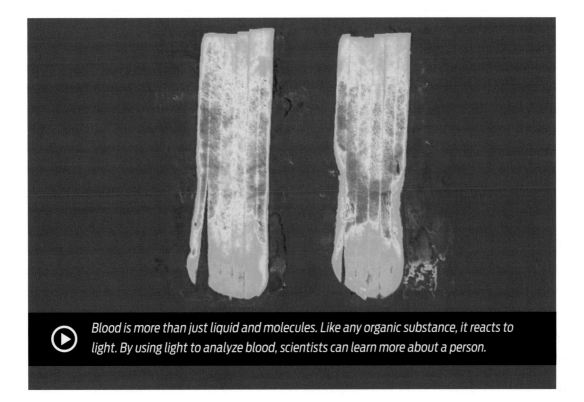

Blood is more than just liquid and molecules. Like any organic substance, it reacts to light. By using light to analyze blood, scientists can learn more about a person.

Why the numbers? At every crime scene, placards like these are photographed showing the location of every bit of evidence, from blood spots to trash.

color wavelengths that can detect pigments of blood in locations that are hard to spot, like on dark rugs, clothing, and furniture.

Moreover, the device allows scientists to age the blood. When blood is first spilled, it is bright red. It then turns a murky brown or rust color over a predictable amount of time. The device analyzes each hue, telling scientists when blood was first shed.

Experts hope the new technology will transform crime scene investigations by speeding up the process of analyzing blood. As it stands now, when police find blood at a crime scene, they must carefully collect the evidence for testing. That means using a gauze pad or a clean cotton cloth to swab wet blood. The blood then has to dry before it is taken to the laboratory for analysis. Hyperspectral imaging will change all that.

"What this does is provide fast, at-the-scene identification of blood and speed up the investigative process, as items do not need to go back to a laboratory to be examined," Islam told a newspaper reporter. "To use hyperspectral imaging in a way that scans the crime scene for blood also means that the chances of missing a bloodstain are vastly reduced."

The technology can also be used with other body fluids, such as saliva and semen.

How is Luminol spray used?

Analyzing Broken Glass

A car crash that shatters the passenger side window of a car. . . broken bottles left near a pool of blood. . . a bullet hole through the backdoor window. Glass fragments can be important pieces of crime scene evidence. Investigators can find glass particles on a victim's clothing, shoes, near a body, or even in the body. Tools, baseball bats, even bullets might contain glass fragments.

Sometimes, if forensic scientists are lucky, they can piece broken glass together like a jigsaw puzzle. They can also compare glass fragments as small as a pinhead. If someone has struck a window with a rock, stick, or a fist, it

Luminol

One of the oldest ways to find invisible blood evidence is to spray a chemical called Luminol, a light-producing chemical that reacts with several substances in blood. A crime scene investigator sprays Luminol on a particular area and then shines a black light on the treated surface. Blood will glow under the black light.

Using Luminol is time-consuming. It doesn't always work, especially when the crime was committed outdoors in sunlight.

is possible to determine the size of the impact and how much force a person used.

Moreover, glass fragments can be easily transferred from victim to suspect and vice versa. Often, glass will be present on a suspect's clothing, tying him or her to a crime. Clothing holds onto glass fragments, making it difficult for a suspect to brush them away.

In the old days, forensic scientists compared glass fragments by looking at color, **density**, surface characteristics, and other properties. They used microscopes, X-ray machines, and other techniques. All were okay in their day, but they could not tell investigators the chemical or physical nature of materials that looked similar.

Forensic experts study images like this one, and the resulting pattern of broken glass created, to help understand the motion, path, and direction of bullets.

That's all changed thanks to a new technology that can analyze and compare traces of glass right down to its atomic structure. The process has an unwieldy name: Laser Ablation Inductively Coupled Plasma Mass Spectrometry, or LAICPMS, for short.

During a crime scene investigation, scientists can take glass and put it through a highly sensitive machine that quickly performs a number of tests. A laser **vaporizes** a bit of the glass sample, turning it into a gas. The gas is then pumped through a mass spectrometer for analysis.

The technology allows scientists to find and analyze the smallest samples of glass, clothing fibers, and other materials. Moreover, LAICPMS damages only a tiny bit of the evidence.

Xbox Tech

We live in a digital world. Digital information is on our computers, smartphones, tablets, and iPads. Each is a great place to store photos, videos, audios, and text files. Often, criminals store illegal material on these devices. There is also another hiding place that criminals use—video-game consoles, including Xbox.

Michael Collins has spent a lot of time figuring out how to look through Xbox and other gaming consoles to unearth evidence that might escape police. Although game consoles might not seem a likely hiding place for illegal material, Collins knows better.

"Once the Xbox file system is mounted, the analyst can browse the directory tree, list its contents, open and view files, and expand subdirectories and files," Collins explained to a reporter.

Why would anyone hide illicit data on their Xbox? The reason is simple, Collins said. Police would not normally look there, especially if a suspect has a smartphone and computer that police can check.

Collins has received requests from the Federal Bureau of Investigation, the U.S. Defense Cybercrime Center, and the Texas State Attorney General's office to use his "toolkit."

The Hunt for Fingerprints

Fingerprints have been the curse of criminals for decades. The unique series of lines, ridges, loops, and curves has sent many people to the death chamber and many more to prison. Since no two fingerprints are alike, if one is found at a crime scene, chances are that person has some explaining to do.

People leave fingerprints on windowpanes, doorknobs, guns, knives, drinking glasses, tables, and other surfaces, including fabric. While it is easy to pluck a fingerprint from the surface of a glass, gun, or knife, trying to find a fingerprint on a blanket, shirt, or sheet is impossible.

Or is it?

Scientists at the University of Abertay Dundee in Scotland have figured out a way to lift fingerprints from cloth using a technology known as Vacuum Metal Deposition (VMD). The process

Is this a murder weapon? The fingerprints being lifted—after powder is applied and sticks to oily residue—might provide the answer.

is already being used to find hidden fingerprints on magazine pages, garbage bags, and other plastic surfaces.

VMD involves coating surfaces with a thin film of gold and zinc. Investigators heat the metals in a vacuum and allow them to evaporate. The result is a high-quality fingerprint image.

Scientists hope the process can find fingerprints on fabric. They have been successful in several experiments. They place a piece of cloth in a vacuum chamber and begin melting gold until it starts

Fingerprints Don't Lie

Why is it that criminals leave fingerprints in the first place? Just beneath the skin of the human hand and fingers are sweat glands. Those sweat glands ooze oils through tiny holes known as pores. The oil mixes with perspiration. When a person touches a surface, it creates an image of a finger on the object.

to evaporate. When the gold is hot enough, scientists spread a thin layer of it over the fabric. They then heat up zinc. The molten metal attaches to the gold, revealing the fingerprint.

"It is like a photographic negative, where colors show up as their opposites," explained Joanna Fraser, a forensic science researcher at the university. "Here the fingerprint ridges show through as clear fabric, but where there are no ridges we see the distinctive gray color of the metal."

The technique seems to work well on cloth woven from a high number of threads. Scientists have also recovered identifiable fingerprints on silk, nylon, and polyester. Moreover, VMD can allow forensic scientists to find a possible fingerprint on a piece of fabric and target it for DNA analysis.

Nanoparticles and Fingerprints

Scientists are working on other ways to find and analyze fingerprints. Swiss researchers say that nanoparticles, microscopic objects that are less than 100 nanometers wide, are drawn to fingerprints by a chemical reaction. The tiny particles, it seems, bond with the compounds in the residue of a fingerprint mark. The researchers can use this knowledge to target previously undetectable fingerprints at the scene of a crime.

Researchers at the University of Lausanne put a series of fingerprints onto a sheet of aluminum foil. They then put the foil in a solution of silicon dioxide particles. Silicon dioxide, better known as silica, is a natural compound and one of the most abundant minerals on the planet.

Scientists coated the silicon dioxide particles with chemicals containing carbon, hydrogen and oxygen. Scientists then took a special dye and put it in the solution. When scientists turned on a special light, they saw the fingerprints emerge. The nanoparticles were attracted to the amino acids and proteins in the residue of the fingerprint. Amino acids are small molecules that are one of the building blocks of protein.

"Since one chemical group from the fingermark residue has been targeted, others can be targeted as well, thus multiplying the chances of detecting previously undetectable fingermarks," said lead researcher Sebastien Moret.

Forensic Spray Glue

Identifying a burn victim can be a time-consuming and grisly task. When a person dies in a house fire, car crash, or plane crash, it is nearly impossible to identify visually who it might be. DNA

Brain Waves

Even the brain has a type of fingerprint. To find it, police hook a suspect up to a machine that records brain waves. Police then ask a series of questions about the crime. As the suspect listens, a computer interprets the electric signals given off by his or her brain. The device will show a positive response when the right question is asked. Some researchers think brain fingerprints are pseudo, or fake, science. They say there are a number of flaws with the technology and the way police question suspects.

and fingerprints melt away when temperature exceeds 482°F (250°C). Teeth, however, are the toughest part of the human body. When a victim is severely burned, dental remains are the most reliable way to identify a person.

"When examining a burn victim's dental remains, we look at things like fillings, crowns, and roots," said Dr. John Berketa, from the University of Adelaide in Australia. "We also look at the distance between teeth, the size of roots and teeth, and their curvatures. We compare all of this information with dental records to identify a deceased person."

When bodies are moved or transported, teeth can fall apart, making it harder to identify a victim. Berketa, however, has developed a

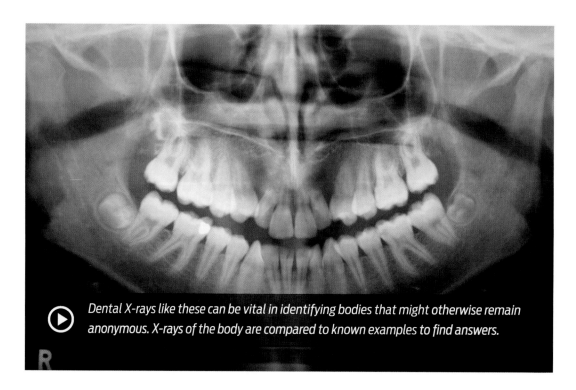

Dental X-rays like these can be vital in identifying bodies that might otherwise remain anonymous. X-rays of the body are compared to known examples to find answers.

R

type of spray that police can carry and spray on the mouths of burn victims. The spray acts like a glue and stabilizes the teeth of the victim so they don't shatter, crack, or fall out.

"This will make the job of forensic dentists much easier and will reduce errors and delays when it comes to providing the coroner and family and friends with a victim's identity," Berketa said.

 ## Text-Dependent Questions

1. What does hyperspectral imaging look for?

2. What is Luminol, and how does it work?

3. What does vacuum metal deposition detect?

 ## Research Project

Break off into groups of three or four. Have each person rub a small amount of lotion onto one thumb. Each person should put his or her thumbprint on a drinking glass. Sprinkle a small amount of powder on the glass. Brush away the excess powder. Place a piece of clear tape over each print and stick them on a black piece of paper.

Next, have each person rub a pencil on his or her thumb. Have everyone press their thumbs on white paper. Label each print. Compare the prints from the glass to those on the white paper. Can you figure out which print belongs to which person?

From microscopic DNA and tiny fingerprints to massive skid marks and blocks-long accident scenes, forensic science takes on all sizes of evidential challenges.

ENGINEERING AND
Forensics

> ## Words to Understand
>
> **infallible**   incapable of failing or being incorrect
>
> **migrated**   moved
>
> **paramedics**   emergency medical workers
>
> **polymer**   a compound with flexible long chains of molecules
>
> **trusses**   support to strengthen a roof, bridge, building, or some other structure

Goldie Alley and her husband, Max, were driving on Interstate 40 in Oklahoma on their way from the town of Broken Arrow to Arkhoma. They were on their way to church. At about 7:45 A.M., a section of a bridge spanning the Arkansas River gave way, sending their truck plummeting to the river, 30 feet (9.1 m) below. Luckily, their car came to rest on a lower portion of the span, just 8 feet (2.4 m) from the river.

"There was a big ol' truck on our side and he would have…been on top of us and we would have been smashed," Alley said.

This deadly bridge collapse led to a massive investigation that included structural engineers, architects, and forensic engineers.

Fourteen people died and five others were injured that day when a 580-foot (176.78 m) section of the bridge broke loose. No one knew at the time why the bridge gave way. Shortly after the incident, a team of forensic engineers began to piece together what happened. Like detectives at a crime scene, the engineers poured over evidence to determine why the span fell.

They eventually figured out that a towboat and two barges traveling upstream on the river collided with one of the bridge's piers. The captain of the tugboat passed out, losing control of his vessel and slamming into the bridge. "I remember looking out to the side of the buoy and then looking back at the bridge, and after that I don't remember nothing," the captain told investigators.

Investigators determined the tugboat and barges rammed into the unprotected piers of the bridge, knocking down two pieces and damaging another. The impact caused four of the bridge's approach spans to collapse.

Their investigation forced the state to install 70 pier protectors at the I-40 bridge and other spans across Oklahoma. Pier protectors are steel cylinders that rise out of the water, creating a protective barrier between bridges and anything headed their way.

Not only do forensic engineers study why bridges collapse, but they also investigate why other structures fail. Like forensic scientists and crime scene investigators, forensic engineers collect and analyze evidence to determine the why and how of a mishap. Their testimony is often used in criminal and civil court cases. What they find can change the way buildings, bridges, and other structures are built.

World Trade Center

Perhaps the greatest forensic engineering investigation was the World Trade Center collapse in 2001. The Twin Towers in New York City fell after terrorists flew planes into the two buildings. When the towers collapsed, it destroyed a lot of evidence that forensic engineers would have liked to examine.

Nevertheless, more than 200 investigators sifted through the debris and collected as much evidence as they could find. They looked at 236 pieces of steel, 7,000 photographs, and 7,000 segments of video. They also interviewed more than 1,000 people

Inside a forensic engineering unit

who were at the site or who had helped build the towers. They then painstakingly re-created every moment that led to the towers' destruction.

The engineers developed a computer model that showed the damage each tower sustained, how fuel from the jets dispersed, and how the resulting fire spread across each floor. They learned how the steel in the structure heated and weakened. Several times, the engineers had to invent new models to explain things they had never seen before.

They finally discovered that the impact of the planes dislodged the fireproofing insulation that coated steel **trusses** and columns, leaving the metal unprotected.

As the fire raged, its intense heat (upwards of 1,800°F/1,000°C) weakened the bare steel. The floors sagged and pulled the columns around the building inward, ultimately resulting in the buildings' collapse. It took three years for forensic engineers to detail the tragedy. The engineers applied what they learned and issued 31 recommendations to improve the safety of other skyscrapers.

Fire in the Hole!

Sometimes, forensic engineers are called to determine damage before it occurs. Engineers and investigators from the Washington State Crime Lab and a private company called CASE Forensics

This photo shows the powerful effects of a flash-bang grenade. Army security officers take part in an exercise that prepares them to use the weapons.

wanted to know whether new flash grenades police were using packed the same amount of explosive punch as older flash grenades. They also wanted to know under what conditions the new grenades could start a fire.

Flash grenades are an effective weapon for many law enforcement agencies. The grenades explode with a "bang" and a blinding flash of light. In Washington, police wanted to know if new flash grenades packed with 12 grams of flash powder worked as well

Electrical Forensics

When a faulty appliance or a bad circuit breaker goes haywire and starts a fire, it is the job of the forensic electrical engineer to figure out what happened. Insurance companies often employ forensic electrical engineers to determine the cause of a house or building fire.

Among other things, a forensic electrical engineer will check to see if an appliance—such as a coffee maker, clothes dryer, or refrigerator—malfunctioned, or if an electrical system was improperly installed.

as the older grenades that had 25 grams. They tested and found out the new grenades were just as loud, if not louder.

Could the grenades cause a fire? "There have been major incidents where a flash-bang has caused a fire, but what are the chances of that happening, what's the likelihood of a flash-bang catching something on fire?" Rick Wyant, a state forensic investigator, wanted to know.

It took a while, but experts were able to find the right conditions in which a flash grenade could trigger a fire. For the most part, the flash is very brief and doesn't generate enough energy or heat to ignite most things.

Police also wanted to experiment with tear gas to see if it would catch fire, especially if used with the flash grenades. Forensic engineers placed an open tear-gas canister inside a bucket on which was taped a lit flare. The gas smoldered but never caught fire.

Bioengineering to the Max

Lukis Anderson was a 26-year-old homeless man whose DNA was at the wrong place at the wrong time. It was November 2012, and police had responded to a murder at the home of a millionaire named Raveesh Kumra. Forensic investigators scraped the underside of Kumra's fingernails and unearthed a trove of DNA.

The genes matched Lukis Anderson. But there was one big problem. Anderson was miles away, unconscious in a hospital bed, at the time of the murder. Still, he spent five months in jail as investigators tried to figure out how he could have committed the crime.

The answer was simple: He didn't.

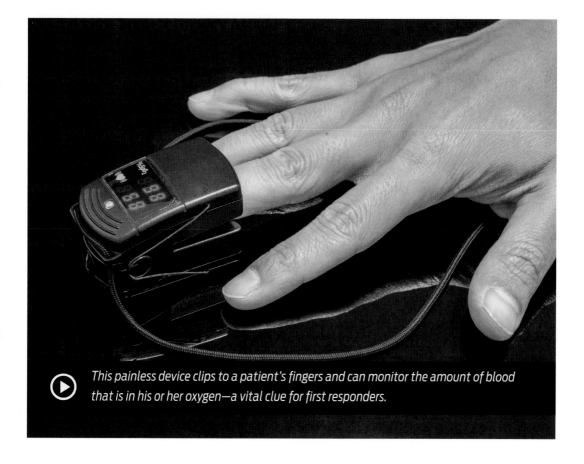

This painless device clips to a patient's fingers and can monitor the amount of blood that is in his or her oxygen—a vital clue for first responders.

In one case, the act of putting a person in an ambulance—and sharing a monitor—was the trigger for an unusual occurrence of evidence migration.

Police finally determined that Anderson and Kumra were transported to the hospital by the same **paramedics**. The first responders had clipped an oxygen monitor to Anderson's finger in the morning. They then clipped the same sensor to Kumra's fingertip in the afternoon. Anderson's DNA somehow **migrated** underneath Kumra's fingertip.

Most people never doubt DNA evidence. But, as the story illustrates, DNA evidence is not **infallible**, nor is it absolute. DNA evidence can be tampered with. It can be mishandled. It can be contaminated.

"The presence of a DNA profile says nothing about the time frame or the circumstances under which it came to be there," said researcher Dan Krane. "Test results can't distinguish between the possibility of contamination, or evidence tampering, or, you know, murder."

That's why engineers are trying to make DNA sequencing as precise as possible.

Next-Generation Sequencing

Inside every DNA laboratory are groups of forensic robots, sequencers whose job it is to isolate and amplify DNA from evidence. The DNA that needs to be sequenced is placed in a gelatin-like substance and put inside the machine. Researchers place electrodes at either end of the gel and then turn on the power. When DNA molecules are electrified, they move through the gel, and separate into different bands. The auto sequencing machine—the forensic robot—reads the order of the DNA bases. Four bases make up DNA. They are adenine (A), guanine (G), thymine (T), and cytosine (C). The sequence of bases (GAC, for instance) is the genetic code. The robot stores this information in its computerized brain.

Today's sequencers can parse about 100 cells, but engineers are working on a group of machines that can extract a DNA profile from just one cell. It's called Next-Generation Sequencing, or

See DNA sequencing in action

NGS for short, and it can cut the time and cost of extracting and sequencing.

One of the newest NGS approaches bio-engineers have developed is strand sequencing. At the heart of the process is a protein nanopore with a tiny hollow tube at its center. The tube is only a few nanometers in diameter, which is smaller than the average bacteria.

A forensic scientist can place a sample of blood or some other bit of evidence into the device. Inside is a silicon chip with a thin **polymer** membrane and the microscopic nanopores. An enzyme "unzips" the twin strands of the DNA molecule into one strand, allowing it to pass through the nanopore.

The device then sends a beam of ions that strike the DNA molecule. A sensor records the electrical disturbances each DNA base makes as it blocks the flowing ions. A computer analyzes the signal, determining the sequence of each base on the entire DNA strand.

It's cheap. It's fast. The implications for law enforcement can be great. Strand sequencing saves time and is more precise than traditional DNA sequencing. But once again, no matter how exact the technology, scientists, police, prosecutors, and defense lawyers still have to figure out what it all means.

"Next-gen sequencing might generate lots of data from small amounts of DNA, but you're still faced with the same fundamental question: What does it mean?" John Butler, who has written several books on DNA analysis, told a reporter, "You could detect a single cell on a knife blade, but that doesn't mean anything—it might have arrived there long before the crime or been transferred there by chance."

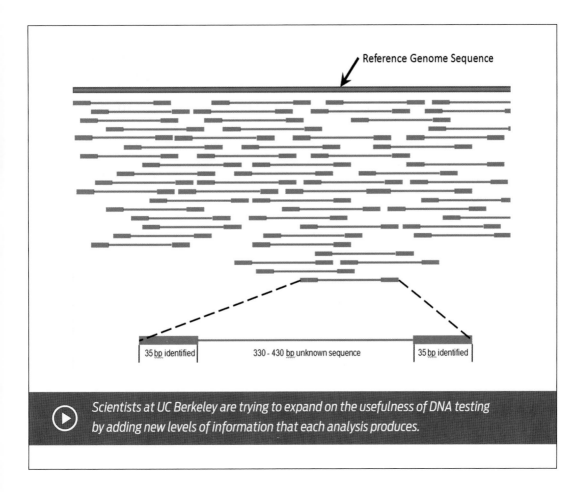

Reference Genome Sequence

| 35 bp identified | 330 - 430 bp unknown sequence | 35 bp identified |

Scientists at UC Berkeley are trying to expand on the usefulness of DNA testing by adding new levels of information that each analysis produces.

A PCR machine like this one translates the DNA codes found in samples provided by forensics teams into DNA results that can match a suspect to a crime.

Speed of Light

Speed is also behind a new DNA amplification technology being studied by bioengineers at the University of California at Berkeley. The engineers have found a way to replicate multiple copies of a specific DNA molecule. The process, called Photonic PCR, heats and cools genetic samples with a flash of light. PCR is short for polymerase chain reaction and it can amplify a single copy of DNA into millions of copies. PCR can be used to diagnose disease, analyze DNA samples from a long-dead mummy, or help put a criminal behind bars.

The technology works when engineers shine light-emitting diodes (LEDs) onto thin films of gold and a DNA solution. The light rapidly heats and cools the gold strip. By repeating and cooling the DNA on the gold strip, the double stranded DNA molecule is replicated many times over. It usually takes an hour or more to amplify DNA, which is much too slow for many applications.

 ## Text-Dependent Questions

1. Explain the job of a forensic electrical engineer.

2. Name three reasons why DNA is not always reliable.

3. How many bases make up DNA?

 ## Research Project

Use the Internet and the library to examine a criminal case in which DNA evidence was used to prosecute a suspect. Write a report on how scientists gathered, analyzed, and presented the DNA evidence. In writing your report, answer these questions: Did the jury find the defendant guilty or not? How did the defense team attack the DNA evidence?

Burglars like this one are often foiled by old-fashioned police work. Today, however, mathematical models also might prove to be the bad guy's undoing.

MATH AND
Forensics

Words to Understand

algorithm   a logical, systematic procedure for solving mathematical problems

attributes   qualities or properties of something or someone

database   a collection of information on a computer

parabola   a mathematical curve shaped like an arc

Burglaries are frustrating crimes and often go unsolved. No community is immune. Burglars tend to be invisible, working at night or when people are not at home. Eyewitnesses who might be able to identify a thief are virtually nonexistent. Many people have come home to a house that has been ransacked and robbed.

In Cambridge, Massachusetts, a group of individuals, including two local crime analysts and a professor and student from the Massachusetts Institute of Technology (MIT), are using math to help solve these crimes.

Crime scene statistics start with anything from interviews with witnesses and victims to patterns of crime locations to the incidence of certain crimes in a neighborhood.

Using a computer and an **algorithm** that the team created, the mathematical sleuths found a way to detect patterns in area burglaries. They have been able to plot the times the crimes took place, how the burglars broke in, where the burglaries took place, and where the homeowner was during the crime.

The algorithm can pore through thousands of bits of information in minutes, spitting out similar crimes and patterns that would otherwise take an investigator days to find on a computer **database**.

"This has the potential to be very significant," Lieutenant Daniel Wagner, who runs the department's crime analysis unit, told the *Boston Globe*. "This tool, if we're able to begin to use it on a daily or a regular basis, would help us identify crime series that we might not have picked up on manually..."

No one has ever been arrested because of the algorithm, but police say it is just a matter of time.

Math to the Max

Math is an important part of our lives, whether we want to admit it or not. Meteorologists use math to predict the weather. Stockbrokers and bond traders use it to make money. We need math to figure out car and mortgage payments. All of us use math to tell time, or to know how much gas to put in our cars. Even police and forensic investigators use math to solve crimes.

In fact, mathematics is fast becoming the most important tool police and forensic investigators have. Whether it is trigonometry, calculus, or vector analysis, math can solve a wide range of problems and crimes. It can determine where a bullet was fired from, why a blood-splatter pattern looks as it does, and if a knife-wielding assailant was left-handed or right-handed.

"Mathematics is important and highly relevant to crime fighting in particular, and to many other real-life problems in general," Professor Chris Budd from the University of Bath told Phys.org. "It won't solve every problem, but mathematics is a particularly useful tool in the set of techniques used in the forensic service."

Hot-Spot Calculations

Jeffrey Brantingham, an anthropologist, and Andrea Bertozzi, a professor of mathematics, have been working with police in Los Angeles trying to build a mathematical model that will help the cops to analyze and categorize urban crime "hot spots." The researchers believe their work will help identify what type of crime is being committed in a particular area, which would give the police an idea of how to combat the criminals.

Brantingham and Bertozzi say their statistical model has found two types of crime hot spots in cities. The first is a "super-critical hot spot" in which there are small upticks in crime. These hot spots are unstable. They come and they go.

The second is a "subcritical hot spot." Criminals gravitate to these areas, creating large spikes in crime. These hot spots are more stable than supercritical hot spots. A large neighborhood drug market that has been there for months or even years is an example of a subcritical hot spot.

The researchers say by knowing the different types of hot spots, police can tailor their response. The mathematical model, which has not yet been put into use, is able to predict how each type of hot spot will respond to an increased police presence.

According to the model, scientists predict that sending more police into a supercritical hot spot does not provide a lasting solution. The criminals will simply move somewhere else.

"If you were to send police into a hot spot without knowing which kind it is, you would not be able to predict whether you will just cause displacement of crime—moving it somewhere else—or whether you will actually reduce crime," Brantingham told a reporter for *U.S. News and World Report.*

Blood Tales

As we said before, blood often plays a central role in forensic investigations. Not only does blood contain a treasure trove of biological information, such as DNA, but the way blood falls, moves, and drips can tell forensic investigators a tale all its own.

By correctly measuring bloodstains and blood splatters, forensic scientists can tell how much force was used to propel the blood forward, or backward, as the case may be. A gunshot wound, for example, will spray small drops of blood over a wide area, while the impact of a baseball bat or hammer will form large drops in more concentrated areas.

Whodunit?

Agatha Christie is the queen of the murder mystery, and trying to figure out who the killer is in any of her books has been a favorite pastime for many. Researchers in Great Britain say that they have come up with a mathematical formula that will identify the culprit every time. Their equation is:

$$k \, r, \delta, \theta, c = f\{rk + \delta + \theta P, M, c(3 \leq 4.5\}.$$

The formula takes into account a variety of **attributes** in every Christie murder mystery, including the relationship (r) of the victim and killer (k); and the type of transportation (δ) central to the plot. One British newspaper tested the formula on Christie's *Crooked House*, which was published in 1949. The formula worked.

While investigators have gotten good at determining the direction the blood came from, they always had a hard time figuring out height. Investigators can use height as a way to tell what position a person was in during an attack. They can determine whether the victim was low to the ground when they were killed, or standing up. Were they sitting? Were they on their backs?

The problem is that blood arcs in a type of mathematical curve called a **parabola**. Blood traveling over different paths from different heights can end at the same angle, making it difficult for forensic scientists to determine height.

Mathematicians have now solved that problem by devising an equation that calculates height by finding an elevation consistent with two blood drops. The equation is written $Z_0 = \frac{(t_1 - t2_2)}{2r_2 - 2r_2}$.

The equation describes how to find the height of the blood drop as it starts its parabolic arc. It takes into account the angles of the first and second blood drop to hit the ground, along with

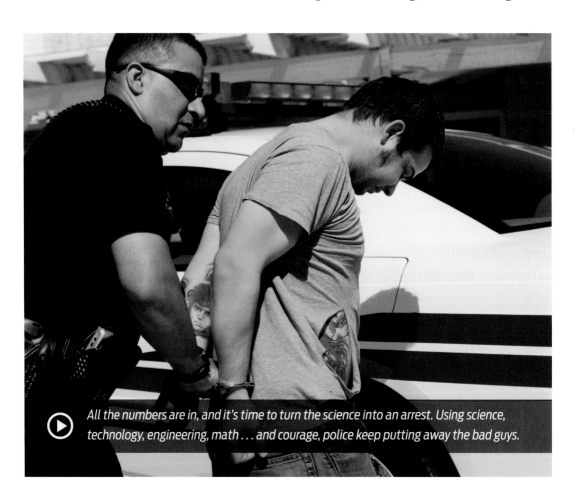

All the numbers are in, and it's time to turn the science into an arrest. Using science, technology, engineering, math . . . and courage, police keep putting away the bad guys.

the distance the first and second drops traveled. By applying the equation, a forensic scientist can say with certainty where a person was positioned when he or she was killed.

From high-tech machines to basic science, from techology that stays one step ahead of crime to math that seals the deal, STEM disciplines are playing a vital role in forensic science. More than ever before, police have science on their side.

 # Text-Dependent Questions

1. Describe the differences between a "subcritical" and a "supercritical" hot spot?

2. Who is Agatha Christie?

3. Why is height important in examining blood-splatter evidence?

 # Research Project

Use newspapers, the Internet, or the library, or visit your local police department to research crime in your state, town, or neighborhood. Create a chart detailing the types of crimes people commit and how often they commit them. What can you determine by studying the list? What crimes are major problems for the community?

Find Out More

Books

Genge, Ngaire, E. *The Forensic Casebook: The Science of Crime Scene Investigation.* Upper Saddle River, N.J.: Ballantine Books, 2002.

Riley, Mike. *Cold Cases Solved: More True Stories of Murders That Took Years or Decades to Solve.* Las Vegas, Nev.: Maica International, 2015.

Saferstein, Richard. *Criminalistics: An Introduction to Forensic Science (10th edition).* New York: Prentice Hall, 2010.

Walker, Pam and Elaine Wood. *Crime Scene Investigation: Real-Life Science Labs for Grades 6–12.* San Francisco: Jossey-Bass, 1998.

Websites

CSI: The Experience
www.csitheexperience.org/

Federal Bureau of Investigation: Kids: How We Investigate
www.fbi.gov/fun-games/kids/kids-investigate

National Institutes of Justice
www.nij.gov/topics/forensics/investigations/pages/welcome.aspx

Science Museum
www.sciencemuseum.org.uk/WhoAmI/FindOutMore/Yourgenes/Whydoscientistsstudygenes/WhatisDNAprofiling/HowcanDNAprofilingsolvecrimes.aspx

U.S. Department of Justice
www.justice.gov/ag/advancing-justice-through-dna-technology-using-dna-solve-crimes

Series Glossary of Key Terms

capacity the amount of a substance that an object can hold or transport

consumption the act of using a product, such as electricity

electrodes a material, often metal, that carries electrical current into or out of a nonmetallic substance

evaporate to change from a liquid to a gas

fossil fuels a fuel in the earth that formed long ago from dead plants and animals

inorganic describing materials that do not contain the element carbon

intermittently not happening in a regular or reliable way

ion an atom or molecule containing an uneven number of electrons and protons, giving a substance either a positive or negative charge

microorganism a tiny living creature visible only under a microscope

nuclear referring to the nucleus, or center, of an atom, or the energy that can be produced by splitting or joining together atoms

organic describing materials or life forms that contain the element carbon; all living things on Earth are organic

piston part of an engine that moves up and down in a tube; its motion causes other parts to move

prototype the first model of a device used for testing; it serves as a design for future models or a finished product

radiation a form of energy found in nature that, in large quantities, can be harmful to living things

reactor a device used to carry out a controlled process that creates nuclear energy

sustainable able to be used without being completely used up, such as sunlight as an energy source

turbines an engine with large blades that turn as liquids or gases pass over them

utility a company chosen by a local government to provide an essential product, such as electricity

Index

Credits

(Dreamstime.com: DT. DollarPhoto: DP) Markobe/DP 6; Leica Geosystems 9; Showface/DT 12; fergregory/DP 15; Oak Ridge National Laboratory 17; Yen-yu Shih/DP 18; gemeinfrei/Wiki inset 21; Tyler Olson/DT 21; photographerlondon/DT 22, 40, 60; Michah Baldwin/flickr 24; Saniphoto/DT 26; SortingExpert/Wikimedia 29; kilukilu/DP 30; Payless Images/Shutterstock 32; Manon Ringuette/DT 35; Jonny Mccullagh/DT 38; Xpds/Wikimedia 42; Randy Montoya/Sandia Lab 45; Hooyah808/DP 47; Hongqi Zhang/DT 48; Suspencewl/Wiki 51; Karl Mumm/Wikimedia 52; Mikael Damkier/DT 54; Katarzyna Bialasiewicz/DT 56.

About the Author

John Perritano is an award-winning journalist, writer, and editor from Southbury, Conn., who has written numerous articles and books on a variety of subjects, including science, sports, history, and culture for such publishers as National Geographic, Scholastic, and Time/Life. His articles have appeared on Discovery.com, Popular Mechanics.com, and other magazines and websites. He holds a master's degree in American History from Western Connecticut State University.